Conte

HORSEMANSHIP COMMITTEE

Chairman

Amelia Morris-Payne
Emal: horsemanshipchairman@pcuk.org

Members

- Lea Allen
- Sue Cheape (Area Representative)
- Janet Douglas
- Elizabeth Hughes
- Andrew James (Area Representative)
- Fran Penn
- Ruth Tarry
- Clare Valori

Sports Officer for Horse and Pony Care: horseandponycare@pcuk.org

Sports Officer for Quiz: quiz@pcuk.org

Contact for Art Competition: art@pcuk.org

The Pony Club
Lowlands Equestrian Centre, Old Warwick Road, Warwick, CV35 7AX
Telephone: 02476 698300
www.pcuk.org

NOTE: Rules which differ from those of 2023 appear in bold type and side-lined (as this note).

Rulebook Verson: 24.1

Photographs in this rulebook used with kind permission from Pete Morris and Ultimate Images.

OBJECTIVES - HORSE AND PONY CARE

The Blue Cross Horse and Pony Care competition features teams of three Members who demonstrate their knowledge and practical horsemanship skills taken from The Pony Club Efficiency Test cards over a number of rounds.

Every eventuality cannot be provided for in these rules. In any unforeseen or exceptional circumstances or any other issue in connection with Horse and Pony Care it is the duty of the relevant Officials to make a decision in a sporting spirit and to approach as nearly as possible the intention of these rules. It is the competitor's responsibility to ensure they are complying with the rules of this competition.

"As a Member of The Pony Club, I stand for the best in sportsmanship as well as in horsemanship. I shall compete for the enjoyment of the game well played and take winning or losing in my stride, remembering that without good manners and good temper, sport loses its cause for being. I shall at all times treat my horse with due consideration."

PART I – HORSE AND PONY CARE DRESS RULES

Dress should be appropriate to a working yard environment. Jodhpurs, boots, gloves and hats are expected. Coats should be available in case of weather change.

1. RECOMMENDED DRESS CODE

- ▶ Pony Club sweatshirt
- ▶ **Gilets/jackets may be worn**
- ▶ **Branch/Centre polo shirts may be worn in the event of warm weather**
- ▶ Membership badge
- ▶ Hat – see rule 2
- ▶ Gloves
- ▶ Correct footwear – see rule 4
- ▶ Jodhpurs/breeches

2. HATS AND HAIR

Hair must be tied back securely, in a safe manner to reduce the risk to hair being caught and prevent scalp injuries.

Members must always wear a protective hat when taking part in the Horse and Pony Care Competition. Only hats to the following specifications are acceptable at any Pony Club activity. The Pony Club is consistent with fellow BEF (British Equestrian) Member bodies in its Standards for Riding Hats. Individual sports may have additional requirements with regard to colour and type. It is strongly recommended that secondhand hats are not purchased.

The hat standards accepted as of 1st January 2024 are detailed in the table below:

Hat Standard	Safety Mark
Snell E2016 & 2021 with the official Snell label and number	
PAS 015: 2011 with BSI Kitemark **or** Inspec IC Mark	

(BS) EN 1384:2023 with BSI Kitemark **or** Inspec IC Mark	
VG1 with BSI Kitemark **or** Inspec IC Mark	
ASTM-F1163 2015 & 2023 with the SEI mark	
AS/NZS 3838, 2006 with SAI Global Mark	

Note: Some hats are dual-badged with different standards. If a hat contains at least one compliant hat standard it is deemed suitable to competition, even if it is additionally labelled with an older standard.

▸ The fit of the hat and the adjustment of the harness are as crucial as the quality. Members are advised to try several makes to find the best fit. The hat should not move on the head when the head is tipped forward. The Pony Club recommends you visit a qualified BETA (British Equestrian Trade Association) fitter.

▸ Hats must be replaced after a severe impact as subsequent protection will be significantly reduced. Hats deteriorate with age and should be replaced after three to five years depending upon the amount of use.

▸ Hats must be worn at all times (including at prize-giving) when mounted with a chinstrap fastened and adjusted so as to prevent movement of the hat in the event of a fall.

Hat Checks and Tagging

The Pony Club and its Branches and Centres will appoint Officials, who are familiar with The Pony Club hat rule, to carry out hat checks and tag each hat that complies with the requirements set out in the hat rule with an Pony Club hat tag. Hats fitted with a Pony Club, British Eventing (BE) or British Riding Club (BRC) hat tag will not need to be checked on subsequent occasions. However, the Pony Club reserves the right to randomly spot check any hat regardless of whether it is already tagged.

Tagging is an external verification of the internal label and indicates that a hat meets the accepted standards. The tag does NOT imply any check of the fit and condition of the hat has been undertaken. It is considered to be the responsibility of the Member's parent(s) / guardian(s) to ensure that their hat complies with the required standards and is tagged before they go to any Pony Club event. Also, they are responsible for ensuring that the manufacturer's guidelines with regard to fit and replacement are followed.

For further information on hat standards, testing and fitting, please refer to the British Equestrian Trade Association (BETA) website: British Equestrian Trade Association - Safety and your head (beta-uk.org)

3. FOOTWEAR

Long boots and Jodhpur boots may be worn. Plain black or brown half chaps may be worn with Jodhpur boots of the same colour. Tassels and fringes are not allowed. For the Horse and Pony Care competition yard boots which are unsuitable for riding but are safe for yard work are permitted. Trainers or other footwear are not permitted.

4. JEWELLERY

The wearing of any sort of jewellery when handling or riding a horse/pony is not recommended and if done at any Pony Club activity, is done at the risk of the member/their parent/guardian. However, to stop any risk of injury, necklaces and bracelets (other than medical bracelets) must be removed, as must larger and more pendulous pieces of jewellery (including those attached to piercings) which create a risk of injury to the body part through which they are secured. For the avoidance of doubt a wristwatch, wedding ring, stock pin worn horizontally and/or a tie clip are permitted.

5. PRIZE GIVING

Competitors must be correctly dressed in their competition clothes, including hats.

PART II – ADMINISTRATIVE RULES FOR HORSE AND PONY CARE AREA COMPETITIONS AND CHAMPIONSHIPS

Some of these rules can also be used for Branch/Centre competitions.

Each Pony Club Area shall organise a qualifying competition. Branches/Centres shall compete within their own Areas.

The competition comprises of a Mini, Junior and Senior competition. All teams can be made up with one member only who has also competed at another level in this year's competition provided they are eligible. Complete teams may not compete at more than one level.

At the Area Competition there should not be a limit to how many teams a Branch or Centre can enter.

The Area Representative in conjunction with the Organiser will appoint an appropriate person to act as the Official Steward at Area competitions.

6. ELIGIBILITY

Mini Competition – Teams to consist of three Members. Ages to be 10 years and under on the 1st January of the competition year, with one Member to be 8 years or under on the 1st January of the competition year.

Junior Competition – Teams to consist of three Members. Ages to be 13 years and under on the 1st January of the competition year, with one Member to be 11 years or under on the 1st January of the competition year.

Senior Competition – Teams to consist of three Members. Ages to be under 25 years on the 1st January of the competition year. One Member to be 16 years and under on the 1st January of the competition year. Of the remaining two Members, one may be between 21 and 24 on the 1st January of the competition year.

7. AREA TEAMS

A Branch/Centre unable to raise a complete team may combine with other Branch/Centres within their Area. Members may only combine with the permissions of their District Commissioners/Centre Proprietors and the Area Representative; fair and objective criteria must be applied when selecting these Members. Area teams are to enable smaller Branches/ Centres to field teams of Members who otherwise would be unable to do so.

An Area Team must comprise of three Members from two or more Branches/Centres e.g. three Branches/Centres with one individual each, two Branches/Centres with two and one individuals. Branches/ Centres should communicate with their Area Representative/Centre Coordinator to form Area Teams.

8. ENTRIES AND NUMBERS TO QUALIFY

a. **Area Competitions:** Entries should be sent, together with the entry fee agreed by the Area Organiser, either to the Organiser directly or via the online entry system. Details to be found in the Area Competition schedule. If a team wishes to withdraw, part of the entry fee may be refunded provided notice is received by the Organiser seven or more days before the competition.

b. The winning team from each section of the Area Competition will qualify for the Championships. Any Area that has 10 or more teams competing in the section will have two guaranteed spaces for the Championship. Any Area that has 15 or more teams competing in the section at the Area Competition is guaranteed three spaces at the Championship. Should space allow, further teams may be invited to the Championships at the Organiser's discretion. Invitations will be made to the Championships by consulting scores and inviting the team that were closest in percentage to their 1st placed team at their relevant Area.

When entering either the Area or the National Championships, team names must be distinguishable. They must include Branch/Centre name, and a simple differentiation e.g A, B, C or a short word if there are more than one team entering. Example: Aberconwy Red.

c. **The Championships:** Entries for teams who have qualified for the Championships should be made via the online entry system.

d. Teams qualifying for the Championships who do not wish to attend must inform the Organiser at Prize giving, or to The Pony Club Office at your earliest convenience in order that the qualification passes to the next highest- placed team that does wish to go.

9. WITHDRAWALS (ALL COMPETITIONS & CHAMPIONSHIPS)

If a Branch or Centre withdraws a team or individual prior to the closing date for a competition, a full refund of entry will be made, less an administration charge. Withdrawals after the closing date for a competition will not be refunded.

10. ABANDONMENT (ALL COMPETITIONS & CHAMPIONSHIPS)

In the event of a competition being abandoned, for whatever reason, a refund of 50% of the entry fee will be given. In such an instance the refund process will be communicated and must be followed.

11. SUBSTITUTIONS

Substitutions must be made before the start of the competition. **One original Area Qualifying member must compete at the Championships, unless extenuating circumstances can be presented to the organiser through the horseandponycare@pcuk.org email address up to the start of the competition.**

Each team can request up to two substitutions, where a replacement eligible member may be entered if an original member is not available to compete. All requests to substitute must be made to the organiser via the horseandponycare@pcuk.org email address up to the start of the competition.

12. PROTESTS OR OBJECTIONS

Apart from the Official Steward, the Area Representative and Officials of the competition, only District Commissioners/Centre Proprietors or their appointed representatives are entitled to lodge protests or objections. Protests must be made in writing and addressed to the Organiser. They must be accompanied by a deposit of £25, which is forfeit unless it is decided that there were good and reasonable grounds for the objection.

Protests or objections must be made not later than thirty minutes after the scores have been published. The Official Steward shall give their decision in the first instance.

If this is not accepted, the Jury of Appeal shall give their decisions after investigation and this decision is final.

Horse & Pony Care

PART III – DIRECTIONS TO ORGANISERS OF HORSE AND PONY CARE CHAMPIONSHIPS, AREA AND FRIENDLY COMPETITION

13. QUESTIONS

Questions must be as practically based as possible. At the Championships some questions will be asked to the youngest Team Member first, this should be done at Area Qualifiers too, to ensure all Members get to answer questions.

a. Minis: Questions to be based on the Care section of the E, D and easier parts of the D+ Efficiency Test cards and Mini Horsemanship Achievement Badges. At the Championships a small number of questions will cover all of the D+ syllabus.

b. Juniors: Questions to be based on the Care section of the D, D+, C and easier parts of the C+ Efficiency Test cards and Horsemanship Achievement Badges. At the Championships a small number of questions will cover Advanced Achievement Badges and all of the C+ syllabus.

c. Seniors: Questions to be based on the Care section of the C+, B and AH Efficiency Test cards. Questions at AH Test level should be used sparingly as not all Branches/Centres will have AH Test level competitors.

NB Centre Members: Centre Members do not own their own ponies, so be aware of this with wording and use open questions such as "How often should a pony be wormed?" rather than "How often should your pony be wormed?"

14. STRUCTURE

- ▸ There should be up to ten stations.
- ▸ Teams rotate with ten minutes at each station for Senior and Junior and eight minutes for Mini.
- ▸ A whistle or bell will be rung with two minutes until the end of the round.
- ▸ A whistle or bell will be rung again to indicate the end of the section.
- ▸ There is a two minute break in between rounds to move to the next table.

- ▸ The start of the next round is indicated by a whistle or a bell.
- ▸ A ten-minute break can be scheduled after five rounds.

A draft score sheet can be found in Appendix B for use at Horse and Pony Care competitions.

15. HORSES AND PONIES

Minis: Ponies under 14.2hh and ideally smaller.

Juniors: Ponies should be under 14.2hh.

Seniors: Horses should be between 14.2hh and 16hh.

16. ASSESSORS

Assessors can be used from local Branches and Centres; the Area Representative may be able to assist in finding suitable assessors.

Minis: Assessors should be familiar with D+ Test standard.

Juniors: Assessors should be familiar with C+ Test standard.

Seniors: Assessors should be familiar with AH Test standard.

17. RESULTS AND SCORING

Organisers are advised to hold a briefing for Assessors at the beginning of the day to ensure they are clear on timings and how to complete score sheets. **Each round will be scored out of 50.**

Tie Breaker: All competitors are required to attend a briefing before the competition. **Three sections, in the order in which they will apply, must be identified in advance and announced at the competitor briefing as the Tie Break Rounds,** to prepare for **a tie between two or more teams.** The briefing will also include an explanation of the tie break round.

There will no longer be a teamwork score /5 per round.

Branches and Centres are judged together and not split into two sections.

Area Competitions **must** be recorded on Pony Club Results.

Area Competitions should be finished by 1st July unless permission is granted by The Pony Club Office.

Full results must be added to Pony Club Results within 7 days of the Area Competition taking place. If you are unable to use Pony Club Results you need to contact The Pony Club Office before the Area Competition and must return full results within 7 days of the Area Competition taking place.

Contact details for the Team Managers of the qualified teams should be provided; they will be contacted directly once the online event entry system is open for the Championships.

At the end of the competition, 30 minutes before the results are finalised, scoresheets must be returned to the Team Manager.

At the end of the competition, Team Managers will have 15 minutes to check the provisional score sheet and put in any objections.

Mini Competition: Although the Mini competition should be run in the same way as the Juniors/Seniors, a 'friendly' emphasis should be used to encourage future participation.

18. PRIZES

a. AREA COMPETITIONS

- All competitors in the Mini Competition should recieve a "special" rosette if not placed.
- **All placed teams must recieve a rosette for each competitor.**
- **It is recommended that rosettes are given to 10th place.**
- It is recommended that a "Best Individual" award is presented to an outstanding individual in each level of competition.

b. CHAMPIONSHIPS

- **At the Championships, all competitors who attend will receive a rosette from the sponsor, Blue Cross.**
- **All competitors will also receive a Championship Plaque.**
- A 'Best Individual' Award will be awarded to an outstanding individual in each level of competition.
- **Best Individual will be placed 1st-3rd at the Championships in each level of competition.**

19. ORGANISER SUPPORT

The following webinars will take place to support the areas to hold an organised Horse and Pony Care competition at the correct standard.

These will be carried out every year at the start of the year and will be available to watch on YouTube afterwards.

a. AREA ORGANISERS

16th January 2024, 6:30pm

This webinar is for the organisers of the area competitions. This will cover:

- Running the competition
- Assessors
- Questions
- Scoring
- Rules
- Rosettes
- Qualifiers
- Results

b. TRAINERS/PARENTS/MEMBERS

24th January 2024, 6:30pm

This webinar is for anyone that would like to know about Horse and Pony Care. This will cover:

- What is Horse and Pony Care
- Running of the day
- Questions
- Assessors
- Training and Teams
- Rules
- Qualification
- Results
- Champs

c. ASSESSOR TRAINING

30th January 2024, 6:30pm

This webinar is for anyone that is/could be assessing Horse and Pony Care. This will cover:

- How to prepare to be an assessor
- How to manage your time during the assessment
- How to objectively assess the answers

20. MEDICAL SUSPENSION

If a Member has been suspended from taking part in any activity/competition/sport for medical reasons, this suspension must apply to all Pony Club activities until such time as the Member is passed fit by a medical professional to take part. It is the Member's and parent/guardian's responsibility to ensure adherence to this rule.

Medical letters are required, following a suspension for medical reasons, to allow a Member to take part in any activity again. The letter should be issued by either the hospital or specialist(s) involved in treating the injury, where appropriate.

21. UNSEEMLY BEHAVIOUR

Unseemly behaviour on the part of competitors, parents, team officials or team supporters will be reported as soon as possible by the Official Steward to The Pony Club Office. Offenders may be penalised by disqualification of the Branch/Centre or Branches/Centres concerned for a period of up to three years. Any competitor who, in the opinion of the Official Steward, has been rude or aggressive towards any officials or competitors at a competition, or who has behaved in an aggressive or unfair manner to any horse, may be disqualified.

22. INSURANCE

The Pony Club 'Public and Products Liability Insurance' Policy includes cover for all the official Area Competitions and the Championships. Details of this insurance are available on The Pony Club website.

In the event of any accident, loss or damage occurring to a third party or to the property of a third party (including the general public and competitors) no liability should be admitted, and full details should be sent at once to The Pony Club Office.

The following statements should be included in all event schedules:

Health & Safety

Organisers of this event have taken reasonable precautions to ensure the health and safety of everyone present. For these measures to be effective, everyone must take all reasonable precautions to avoid and prevent accidents occurring and must obey the instructions of the organisers and all the officials and stewards.

Legal Liability

Save for the death or personal injury caused by the negligence of the organisers, or anyone for whom they are in law responsible, neither the organisers of this event or The Pony Club nor any agent, employee or representative of these bodies, nor the landlord or his tenant, accepts any liability for any accident, loss, damage, injury or illness to horses, owners, riders, spectators, land, cars, their contents and accessories, or any other person or property whatsoever. Entries are only accepted on this basis.

OBJECTIVES - QUIZ

The Dodson and Horrell Quiz competition features teams of **three or** four Members who demonstrate their knowledge of Horsemanship in the form of answering questions and playing games with all questions taken from The Pony Club Efficiency Test cards syllabi and Pony Club Badges over a number of rounds.

The Pony Club International Alliance (PCIA) holds an International Quiz either online or in-person annually. The members chosen to represent PCUK are selected from successful Quiz and Horse and Pony Care Teams. Please see Appendix D for the Eligibility Criteria and further information.

Every eventuality cannot be provided for in these rules. In any unforeseen or exceptional circumstances or any other issue in connection with Horse and Pony Care it is the duty of the relevant Officials to make a decision in a sporting spirit and to approach as nearly as possible the intention of these rules. It is the competitor's responsibility to ensure they are complying with the rules of this competition.

"As a Member of The Pony Club, I stand for the best in sportsmanship as well as in horsemanship. I shall compete for the enjoyment of the game well played and take winning or losing in my stride, remembering that without good manners and good temper, sport loses its cause for being. I shall at all times treat my horse with due consideration."

PART IV – QUIZ DRESS RULES

23. RECOMMENDED DRESS CODE

- ▸ Pony Club sweatshirt/polo shirt/jacket (shirt and tie not compulsory
- ▸ Comfortable trousers and footwear (no ripped jeans)

PART V - ADMINISTRATIVE RULES FOR THE QUIZ AREA COMPETITIONS AND FINAL

Some of these rules can also be used for Branch/Centre competitions.

Each Pony Club Area shall organise a qualifying competition. Branches/Centres shall compete within their own Areas.

The competition comprises of a Mini and Junior/Senior competition. All teams can be made up with one member only who has also competed at another level in this year's competition provided they are eligible. Complete teams may not compete at more than one level.

The Area Representative in conjunction with the Organiser will appoint an appropriate person to act as the Official Steward at Area competitions.

24. ELIGIBILITY

Mini Section - Teams to consist of four members. Ages to be 10 years and under on the 1st January of the competition year with one member to be 8 years and under on the 1st January of the competition year.

Junior/Senior Section - Teams to consist of four members. Teams must have two Junior members who are 13 years and under on the 1st January of the competition year and two members of any age up to 25 years on the 1st January of the competition year.

If branch/centre cannot get a 4th member then teams of three are allowed but the following rules apply:

Mini Section - Ages to be 10 years and under on the 1st January of the competition year with one member to be 8 years and under on the 1st January of the competition year.

Junior/Senior Section – Teams must have one member who is 13 years and under on the 1st January of the competition year, the other two members can be any age up to 25 years old on the 1st January of the competition year.

25. AREA TEAMS

A Branch/Centre unable to raise a complete team may combine with other Branch/Centres within their Area. Members may only combine with the permissions of their District Commissioners / Centre Proprietors and the

Area Representative; fair and objective criteria must be applied when selecting these Members. Area teams are to enable smaller Branches/Centres to field teams of Members who otherwise would be unable to do so.

An Area Team must comprise of 3 or 4 members from 2 or more Branches/Centres. e.g. 4 Branches/Centres with one individual each. 3 Branches/Centres with one two and two individuals etc. Branches/Centres should communicate with their Area Representative/Area Centre Coordinator to form area teams.

The spirit of this rule is to allow Branch/Centres to field a team where they otherwise would not have been able to, it is not to allow large Branch/Centres to enable extra competitors to take part or to create potential "super teams".

26. ENTRIES AND NUMBERS TO QUALIFY

Area Competitions: Entries should be sent, together with the entry fee agreed by the Area Organiser, either to the Organiser directly or via the online entry system. Details to be found in the Area Competition schedule. There should not be a limit to how many teams a Branch or Centre can enter.

When entering either the Area or the National Championships, team names must be distinguishable. They must include Branch/Centre name, and a simple differentiation e.g A, B, C or a short word if there are more than one team entering. Example: Aberconwy Red.

At the Area Competitions, both Branch and Centre teams will compete together in one section.

The highest place Branch AND Centre will qualify for the National Final. Additionally, any area that has 10 or more teams competing in the whole section (Branch and Centre together) will receive an additional qualifying space for the National Final. Any area that has 15 or more teams competing in the whole section (Branch and Centre together) will receive two additional qualifying spaces for the National Final. If the highest placed Branch or Centre from the area is not in a qualifying space, they will also receive a qualifying space. After the highest placed Branch and Centre teams, additional qualifying spaces will be awarded based on the scores that were closest to the team placed 1st, regardless of Branch or Centre. Should space allow, further teams may be invited to the National Final at

the Organiser's discretion. 'Extra invites' will be invited to the National Final by consulting scores and inviting the team that were closest in percentage to their 1st placed team at their relevant Area.

The National Final: Entries for teams who have qualified for the National Final should be made via the online entry system.

Teams qualifying for the National Final who do not wish to attend must inform the Organiser at Prize giving, or to The Pony Club Office at your earliest convenience in order that the qualification passes to the next highest- placed team that does wish to go.

27. WITHDRAWALS (ALL COMPETITIONS & NATIONAL FINAL)

If a Branch or Centre withdraws a team or individual prior to the closing date for a competition, a full refund of entry fees will be made, less an administration charge. Withdrawals after the closing date for a competition will not be refunded.

28. ABANDONMENT (ALL COMPETITIONS & NATIONAL FINAL)

In the event of a competition being abandoned, for whatever reason, a refund of 50% of the entry fee will be given. In such an instance the refund process will be communicated and must be followed.

29. SUBSTITUTIONS

Substitutions must be made before the start of the competition. One original Area Qualifying member must compete at the National Final, unless extenuating circumstances can be presented to the organiser through the quiz@pcuk.org email address up to the start of the competition.

Each team can request up to two substitutions, where a replacement eligible member may be entered if an original member is not available to compete. All requests to substitute must be made to the organiser via the quiz@pcuk.org email address up to the start of the competition.

30. PROTESTS OR OBJECTIONS

Apart from the Official Steward, the Area Representative and Officials of the competition, only District Commissioners/Centre Proprietors or their appointed representatives are entitled to lodge protests or objections. Protests must be made in writing and addressed to the Organiser. They must be accompanied by a deposit of £25, which is forfeit unless it is decided that there were good and reasonable grounds for the objection.

Protests or objections must be made not later than thirty minutes after the scores have been published. The Official Steward shall give their decision in the first instance. If this is not accepted, the Jury of Appeal shall give their decisions after investigation and this decision is final.

PART VI – DIRECTIONS TO ORGANISERS OF QUIZ FINAL, AREA AND FRIENDLY COMPETITIONS

31. QUESTIONS

Questions for Area competition will be provided by the Horsemanship Committee along with guidance on scoring. The questions will be formatted as mix of Questions, Activity games, Word games and Identification rounds.

a. MINI SECTION:

Questions will be based on the Care and Riding sections of the E,D and easier parts of the D+ Efficiency Test cards and Mini Horsemanship Achievement badges. At the Final a number of questions will cover all of the D+ syllabus.

b. JUNIOR/SENIOR SECTION:

Questions will be based on the Care and Riding sections of the D+, C & C+ and easier parts of the B Efficiency Test cards, and achievement badges. At the Final a number of questions will cover advanced achievement badges and all of the B syllabus.

32. ROUNDS

The Committee will provide a list of 10 rounds for Mini and 12 for Junior/Senior. Some will be compulsory others will be optional.

Area Competitions:

▸ Area Competitions for 2024 must be on the **3rd March 2024**.
▸ All of the Area rounds will be selected from the list provided.
▸ The Area/Friendly competition should be 6 rounds for Minis.
▸ The Area/Friendly competition should be 8 rounds for Junior/Senior.
▸ Chosen rounds will not be disclosed prior to the start of the competition.
▸ It is up to the area organiser to add extra rounds from the round list provided by the Committee.
▸ One round must be run as an individual round.
▸ All Area competitions will be intended to commence on the same date.

- ► If an area cannot hold the event on this date, they will need to provide their own questions from the list of rounds provided by the Committee.

National Final:

- ► All of the National Final rounds will be selected from the list provided.
- ► All questions and content will be rewritten.
- ► Round names will not be disclosed prior to the start of the competition.
- ► The National Final competition will have 8 rounds for the Mini and Junior/Senior Competitions.

33. STRUCTURE

- ► Teams rotate with 8 minutes per round for Minis and Junior/Senior.
- ► A whistle or bell will be rung with two minutes until the end of the round.
- ► A whistle or bell will be rung again to indicate the end of the round.
- ► There is a 2-minute break in between to move to the next table.
- ► The start of the next round is indicated by a whistle or a bell.
- ► A 10-minute break can be scheduled after five rounds.

34. ROUND TYPES

Minis:

- ► The two supplied question rounds.
- ► Two of the supplied Activity games (one must be Charades)
- ► One of the Word games
- ► One of the ID rounds (to be run as individual round)
- ► Total minimum rounds = 6

Juniors/Seniors:

- ► Two of the supplied Question rounds (one must be The Pony Club)
- ► Two of the supplied Activity games (one must be Pictionary)
- ► Two of the supplied Word games
- ► Two of the supplied ID rounds (One to be run as individual round)
- ► Total minimum rounds = 8

Tie break rounds are to be the question rounds.

The quiz requires a significant number of volunteer helpers to run each table/round. It is recommended that as a condition of entry each team provides at least one helper. Each table requires one helper to run the round, the activity games each require two helpers.

All the information, score sheets, question sheets, answer legends, guidance for running the rounds and equipment list is in individual documents to be found on a Dropbox link sent to the area organiser one month prior to the area competition date. There is one week for organisers to download the information before the Dropbox link expires. If organisers are unable to download all the files in that time contact quiz@pcuk.org or the Pony Club Office and a further Dropbox link will be issued.

35. RESULTS AND SCORING

Organisers are advised to hold a briefing for the scorers and round helpers at the beginning of the day to ensure they are clear on timings and how to complete score sheets. **Each round will be scored out of 50.**

All competitors are required to attend a briefing before the competition. The briefing will include an explanation of the tie break round.

The **highest placed** Branch and Centre from each section get a qualifying place at the National Quiz Final. Should space allow, further teams may be invited to the Championships at the Organiser's discretion. Invitations will be invited to the Championships by consulting scores and inviting the team that were closest in percentage to their 1st placed team at their relevant Area.

Area Competitions **must** be recorded on Pony Club Results. You should name your rounds 1,2,3 etc until the competition has finished so teams do not know the rounds you have picked for the competition.

Area Competitions for 2024 need to be on the 3rd March 2024.

Full results must be added to Pony Club Results within 7 days of the Area Competition taking place. If you are unable to use Pony Club Results you need to contact The Pony Club Office before the Area Competition and must return full results within 7 days of the Area Competition taking place.

It is recommended that organisers have 3/4 dedicated scorers who each have a copy of the questions and answer legend. If possible each scorer should score their round/s from start to finish to ensure consistency.

Rounds will be scored out of a possible 50 points. The weighting of the questions will be related to their difficulty.

Individual rounds will be scored individually out of 50. The best 3 scores for each team will be averaged to create an overall team score. In the event of a 3 person team, all scores will count.

At the end of the competition, **only** the Team Manager/Representative will have 15 minutes to check the provisional score sheet and put in any objections.

Mini competition: Although the Mini competition should be run in the same way as the Juniors/Seniors, a 'friendly' emphasis should be used to encourage future participation.

36. PRIZES

All competitors in the Mini Competition should receive a 'Special' rosette if not placed.

At the National Quiz Final, all competitors who attend will receive a plaque and each section will receive rosettes 1st-10th place.

37. ORGANISER SUPPORT

The following webinars will take place to support the areas to hold an organised Quiz competition at the correct standard.

These will be carried out every year at the start of the year and will be available to watch on YouTube afterwards.

a. Area Organisers

This webinar is for the organisers of the area competitions. This will cover:

- Running the competition
- Rounds
- Scoring
- Rules
- Rosettes
- Qualifiers
- Results

b. Trainers/Parents/Members

This webinar is for anyone that would like to know about Quiz. This will cover:

- What is the Pony Club Quiz
- Running of the day
- Rounds
- Training and Teams
- Rules

- ► Qualification
- ► Results
- ► National Final

38. MEDICAL SUSPENSION

If a Member has been suspended from taking part in any activity/ competition/sport for medical reasons, this suspension must apply to all Pony Club activities until such time as the Member is passed fit by a medical professional to take part. It is the Member's and parent/guardian's responsibility to ensure adherence to this rule.

Medical letters are required, following a suspension for medical reasons, to allow a Member to take part in any activity again. The letter should be issued by either the hospital or specialist(s) involved in treating the injury, where appropriate.

39. UNSEEMLY BEHAVIOUR

Unseemly behaviour on the part of competitors, parents, team officials or team supporters will be reported as soon as possible by the Official Steward to The Pony Club Office. Offenders may be penalised by disqualification

of the Branch/Centre or Branches/Centres concerned for a period of up to three years. Any competitor who, in the opinion of the Official Steward, has been rude or aggressive towards any officials or competitors at a competition, or who has behaved in an aggressive or unfair manner to any horse, may be disqualified.

40. INSURANCE

The Pony Club 'Public and Products Liability Insurance' Policy includes cover for all the official Area Competitions and the Championships. Details of this insurance are available on The Pony Club website.

In the event of any accident, loss or damage occurring to a third party or to the property of a third party (including the general public and competitors) no liability should be admitted, and full details should be sent at once to The Pony Club Office.

The following statements should be included in all event schedules:

Health & Safety

Organisers of this event have taken reasonable precautions to ensure the

Quiz

health and safety of everyone present. For these measures to be effective, everyone must take all reasonable precautions to avoid and prevent accidents occurring and must obey the instructions of the organisers and all the officials and stewards.

Legal Liability

Save for the death or personal injury caused by the negligence of the organisers, or anyone for whom they are in law responsible, neither the organisers of this event or The Pony Club nor any agent, employee or representative of these bodies, nor the landlord or their tenant, accepts any liability for any accident, loss, damage, injury or illness to horses, owners, riders, spectators, land, cars, their contents and accessories, or any other person or property whatsoever. Entries are only accepted on this basis.

PART VII – AREA QUIZ ROUNDS 2024

The rounds for the 2024 Area quiz will be out of the list below:

41. MINI SECTION

QUESTION ROUNDS:

- ▶ The Pony Club
- ▶ Learning Theory

ACTIVITY GAMES

- ▶ Charades (General Knowledge – Based on Rule 31a)
- ▶ Guess the item (Mini Blue Cross Badges)
- ▶ Audio/Visual Game (Handling and Leading)

WORD GAMES

- ▶ Crossword Puzzle (Care of the Foot)
- ▶ Alphabet Soup (General Knowledge)

IDENTIFICATION ROUNDS

- ▶ Yard Safety
- ▶ Odd One Out (Mini Blue Cross Badges)
- ▶ Points of Tack

Each area must as a minimum do two question rounds, two Activity Games (one must be Charades), and one of each Word Games and ID Rounds. Then pick any additional rounds from any remaining from the list above. Areas need to do a minimum of 6 rounds but more can be used if required.

42. JUNIOR/SENIOR SECTION

QUESTION ROUNDS:

- ▶ The Pony Club
- ▶ Learning Theory
- ▶ Worm Control

ACTIVITY GAMES

- ▶ Pictionary (General Knowledge Based on Rule 31b)
- ▶ Guess the item (Blue Cross Achievement Badges)
- ▶ Taboo (Rugs and Boots/Bandages)

WORD GAMES

- ► Crossword Puzzle (Feeding)
- ► Crazy Horse Parts

IDENTIFICATION ROUNDS

- ► What's my Name (Shoeing)
- ► Odd One Out (Blue Cross Achievement Badges)
- ► Points of Tack
- ► Green Thumb (Grasses, Trees and Poisonous Plants)

Each area must pick two rounds from each category (The Pony Club and Pictionary must be included). Then pick any additional rounds from any remaining on the list. Areas need to do a minimum of 8 rounds but more can be used if required.

PART VIII – NATIONAL QUIZ FINAL ROUNDS 2024

43. MINI SECTION

QUESTION ROUNDS:

- The Pony Club
- Learning Theory

ACTIVITY GAMES

- Charades (General Knowledge – based on Rule 31a)
- Guess the item (Mini Blue Cross Badges)
- Jigsaw Puzzle (One of the new Pony Club Posters)

WORD GAMES

- Hexagonal Tarsia (Mini Blue Cross Badges)
- Alphabet Soup (General Knowledge)

IDENTIFICATION ROUNDS

- Yard Safety
- Odd One Out (Mini Blue Cross Badges)
- Points of Tack

At the National Quiz Final the Mini Competition will be 8 rounds taken from the list above.

44. JUNIOR/SENIOR SECTION

QUESTION ROUNDS:

- The Pony Club
- Learning Theory
- Worm Control

ACTIVITY GAMES

- Pictionary (General Knowledge based on Rule 31b)
- Guess the item (Blue Cross Achievement Badges)
- Taboo (Rugs and Boots/Bandages)
- Jigsaw Puzzle (One of the new Pony Club Posters)

WORD GAMES

- ▸ Crossword Puzzle (Feeding)
- ▸ Hexagonal Tarsia (Blue Cross Achievement Badges)

IDENTIFICATION ROUNDS

- ▸ What's my Job (Shoeing)
- ▸ Odd One Out (Blue Cross Achievement Badges)
- ▸ Points of Tack
- ▸ Green Thumb (Grasses, Trees and Poisonous Plants)

At the National Quiz Final, the Junior/Senior Competition will be 8 rounds taken from the list above.

OBJECTIVES – ART COMPETITION

The Pony Club Art Competition is a Non-Ridden Pony Club competition where members can express their artistic creativity and combine this with their passion for horses and ponies.

Every eventuality cannot be provided for in these rules. In any unforeseen or exceptional circumstances or any other issue in connection with Horse and Pony Care it is the duty of the relevant Officials to make a decision in a sporting spirit and to approach as nearly as possible the intention of these rules. It is the competitor's responsibility to ensure they are complying with the rules of this competition.

"As a Member of The Pony Club, I stand for the best in sportsmanship as well as in horsemanship. I shall compete for the enjoyment of the game well played and take winning or losing in my stride, remembering that without good manners and good temper, sport loses its cause for being. I shall at all times treat my horse with due consideration."

PART IX – ART COMPETITION RULES

45. RULES

Entrants must be a current Member of a Pony Club Branch or Centre in the United Kingdom or part of our International Membership.

Individual Competition: One entry is allowed per person.

Team Competiton: Centres/Branches may enter a piece of collaborative art, contributed to by a minimum of three members (no maximum).

The drawing or painting should have a title suggested by this year's theme of **"Friendship and Adventure"**. It should be a personal memory or idea, and if needed, references should be taken from your own or your family's collection of photos, and not from a magazine or published professional material (i.e. when the copyright for the image belongs to someone else.)

Centres/Branches can enter a piece of collaborative art with the same theme as the Individual competition. This is a chance to work together to create a combined piece of artwork that represents your Branch/Centre, and Friendship and Adventure.

The judges will be looking for a well thought out, well painted or drawn picture that successfully conveys the idea being pictured. They will be looking for originality, a flair for colour or drawing, and good use of materials. **This year we will also accept artwork produced digitally, due to the increased developments in technology we are aware this medium is popular and can produce artwork to a high standard.**

The subject of the work must be equestrian-related.

The piece must be entirely the artist's own work.

By entering the competition, entrants give their express permission to allow their work to be used for publicity if required.

There are three separate age categories: 11 years and Under, 12-16 Years, and 17 Years and Over.

Deadline for entries is midnight **18th February 2024**.

46. GUIDELINES FOR PHOTOGRAPHY

Photograph your work outside in natural light, so the colours are true to life and there aren't any shadows caused by thick paint etc. Get someone to hold it if it is windy, or prop it up against a wall or other object.

If it is on paper, tape it to a board of some kind to hold it flat. Make sure there are no shadows across the work from bushes, washing lines etc. If it is really sunny, angle the picture so that the light is not too bright on the image. Make sure your painting is properly dry or it will shine.

To get a nice photo that is not distorted try to line up all the edges of the artwork with the edges of the picture and try to get close enough to fill the whole of the screen with the picture, especially with a mobile phone which will still focus when it is quite close to the picture. If you have a camera with a zoom stand back to about 1.5 - 2 metres from the picture and zoom in to just the picture cutting out the background that way. If you do this you don't have to edit the picture on the computer and it looks more professional. That way you can be sure you have the best possible photo and the least amount of background which is distracting and will spoil your picture.

Make sure the flash is turned off or this will leave a white blob in the middle of the photo where the flash bounces off your work back at the camera.

47. JUDGING

We have a diverse group of award winning, experienced judges lined up to be part of this competition. The Judges' names will be released throughout October, however please don't discuss or make contact with any of them in regard to your competition entry.

Initial Stage: Judging will be done using the images uploaded to the competition website. A total of five entries in each category will be shortlisted for the final stage of judging, and those entrants will be notified in the month of April 2024.

Finals: The five finalists in each age category will go forward to the final stage where the judging panel will decide upon an overall competition Winner and Runner-up.

Winner: The national winner will have the opportunity to have their artwork displayed within The Pony Club Central Office for visitors to view and at prestigious events. The Pony Club will ensure we recognise the talent of our winner in the best ways possible.

48. PRESENTATION OF WORK

The size of the final drawing/painting must be no larger than A2.

We will be viewing the finalists artwork in person to select the winner.

Art Competition

Therefore, we request the artwork is of a size and medium suitable to post. If you would like to frame your art for this stage that would be advantageous but not necessary.

Entries should be photographed digitally and uploaded to The Pony Club Art Competition portal at artcomp.pcuk.org together with the online entry form. The size of the uploaded image should be a maximum of 4MB (if it is larger, you will need to decrease its size in an image editing program before uploading).

APPENDICIES

49. APPENDIX A - HEAD INJURY AND CONCUSSION

There are strict procedures around the response to concussion.

a) General Advice

Head injuries and concussion can be life changing and fatal. Serious head injuries are usually obvious, but concussion can be very subtle. It may not be immediately apparent but should be taken very seriously.

Members may be asked not to ride by an Official (including a first aider) who believes they may have sustained concussion either at the time of injury or from a previous injury (which may not have been sustained whilst riding). Concussion is difficult to diagnose, and practitioners of all grades must err on the side of caution. Thus, any decision must be respected, and professional medical support is advised to avoid further harm. Ignoring an official's advice about concussion breaches The Pony Club's Code of Conduct.

b) Accidents that could cause head injuries or concussion

Any Member involved in an incident that could cause head injury or concussion at a Pony Club activity (for example, a fall from their horse/pony) should be assessed by the first aid provider in attendance.

Dependent on the level of first aid cover, the exact process of diagnosing will vary depending/based on whether the Member has suffered:

- No head injury/concussion
- Suspected head injury/concussion
- Confirmed head injury/concussion

The process for diagnosing each option is covered in more detail below.

An assessment may make it immediately obvious that there is no cause for concern. Reasonable care should be taken to ensure Members have not sustained a serious head injury or concussion.

c) Unconsciousness

If a Member is unconscious following an incident they should be treated as if they are suffering with a confirmed concussion and the steps in point vii should be followed.

d) Who can diagnose head injury or concussion?

Diagnosis of a head injury or concussion can be carried out by Trained First Aiders, Qualified First Aiders or Medical Professionals officiating at a Pony Club activity. If there is any doubt as to the diagnosis, the Member should see the highest level of first aid cover that is present who should make the diagnosis. If a definite diagnosis is not possible then the Member should be referred to a hospital or a doctor off site for a professional diagnosis.

The member must not ride again until they have been seen by a doctor/hospital.

e) Actions to be taken in the event of a suspected head injury or suspected concussion diagnosis

If a diagnosis of a suspected head injury or concussion is made by a first aider, the parents/guardians should be advised to take the member to hospital.

Any Member who has been diagnosed with a suspected or confirmed head injury/concussion should not be left alone and must be returned to the care of their parents/guardians where appropriate.

If a Member has a suspected head injury/concussion at an activity/competition, organisers should inform the DC/Proprietor to ensure that the rider follows these guidelines.

Once a diagnosis of suspected head injury or concussion is made by the first aid cover present at the activity, then that decision is final. If a Member is advised to see a doctor because of suspected head injury/concussion and the parents/guardians decide not to allow the member to be examined (either at the activity or in hospital), the Member will not be allowed to ride again on the day and should be treated as if they have sustained a confirmed head injury/concussion. Depending on the circumstances, the decision not to allow further examination may be considered a safeguarding issue.

Where a doctor subsequently certifies that a Member does not have or did not suffer a head injury/concussion, and provides evidence that they are satisfied the Member is well enough to resume riding activity, that Member will be treated as if they did not sustain a concussion. Officials will endeavour to assess members in a timely way; however, head injuries can evolve over time, which may lead an official or professional to perform a series of assessments. A Member may miss a phase or part of an event during the assessment process and the Sport Rules for missing that phase or part will apply.

f) Actions to be taken in the event of a confirmed head injury or confirmed concussion

In the event of a confirmed head injury or confirmed concussion diagnosis, the doctor will advise the Member not to ride or take part in any activity that potentially involves hard contact for three weeks. The member may be advised that they could request a review of any ongoing concussion problems by a doctor (with experience in assessing concussion) after 10 days. If that doctor is happy to certify that the Member is not suffering with a concussion, the Member may ride again. Evidence regarding this decision is required, e.g. in the form of a medical letter. If no evidence is provided, the Member should not take part in any Pony Club activity that involves horses/ ponies, whether mounted or unmounted, for at least three weeks after the initial injury.

g) Actions to be taken in the event of a diagnosis of a confirmed or suspected head injuries/concussions outside of Pony Club activities

Ultimately, it is the parent/guardians' responsibility to make a decision about the welfare of their child.

If a Pony Club Official becomes aware that a member has sustained a suspected or confirmed head injury/concussion and has been advised not to take part in any potentially hard contact activities, the Member must not be allowed to take part in any Pony Club activities that involve horses/ponies, whether mounted or unmounted for three weeks, unless appropriate medical evidence of fitness to ride can be provided by parents/ guardians dated at least 10 days after the initial injury.

CONCUSSION FLOWCHART

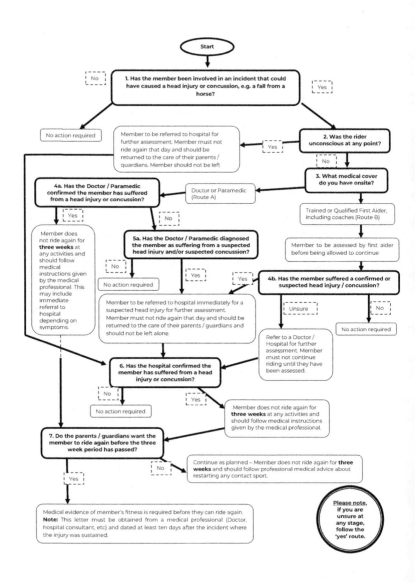

Start

1. Has the member been involved in an incident that could have caused a head injury or concussion, e.g. a fall from a horse?

No

Yes

No action required

Member to be referred to hospital for further assessment. Member must not ride again that day and should be returned to the care of their parents / guardians. Member should not be left

2. Was the rider unconscious at any point?

Yes

No

3. What medical cover do you have onsite?

Doctor or Paramedic (Route A)

Trained or Qualified First Aider, including coaches (Route B)

4a. Has the Doctor / Paramedic confirmed the member has suffered from a head injury or concussion?

Yes

No

Member to be assessed by first aider before being allowed to continue

Member does not ride again for **three weeks** at any activities and should follow medical instructions given by the medical professional. This may include immediate referral to hospital depending on symptoms.

5a. Has the Doctor / Paramedic diagnosed the member as suffering from a suspected head injury and/or suspected concussion?

No

Yes

4b. Has the member suffered a confirmed or suspected head injury / concussion?

Yes

No action required

Member to be referred to hospital immediately for a suspected head injury for further assessment. Member must not ride again that day and should be returned to the care of their parents / guardians and should not be left alone.

Unsure

No

No action required

Refer to a Doctor / Hospital for further assessment. Member must not continue riding until they have been assessed.

6. Has the hospital confirmed the member has suffered from a head injury or concussion?

No

Yes

No action required

Member does not ride again for **three weeks** at any activities and should follow medical instructions given by the medical professional.

7. Do the parents / guardians want the member to ride again before the three week period has passed?

No

Continue as planned – Member does not ride again for **three weeks** and should follow professional medical advice about restarting any contact sport.

Yes

Medical evidence of member's fitness is required before they can ride again. **Note:** This letter must be obtained from a medical professional (Doctor, hospital consultant, etc) and dated at least ten days after the incident where the injury was sustained.

Please note, if you are unsure at any stage, follow the 'yes' route.

50. APPENDIX B - DRAFT SCORE SHEET

The Blue Cross Horse and Pony Care 2024

Team Number:	
Assessor:	

Round 1 –

Questions	Marks Available	Marks Given	Comments
Total	50		
Outstanding Individual			

Please note that the teamwork score has been removed for 2024.

The editable draft scoresheet is available on pcuk.org.

51. APPENDIX C – QUIZ ROUND INFORMATION

Each round will have a total of 50 points available.

All rounds will be considered general knowledge unless they have a specific topic, whenever general knowledge is required it will be taken from the syllabi and badges for the relevant section according to rule 31.

Question Rounds

10 multiple choice questions for Mini.

10 questions requiring written answers for Junior/Senior.

Topics used 2023-24

- ▸ The Pony Club
- ▸ Learning Theory
- ▸ Equine Welfare
- ▸ Equine Safety
- ▸ Worm Control

Activity Games

Guess the Item

Items to be inside a bag, competitors feel through the bag and guess what is inside. Each competitor has 2 minutes and three items to identify. In 2024 items to be selected from the Blue Cross Mini and Achievement badges.

Audio/Visual Game

Clips of film or music to identify either the horse/pony, rider, or what is being done correctly/incorrectly. Topic for 2024 is Handling and Leading

Charades

One team member to act out a word or phrase without using words, which must be guessed by the rest of the team. Each team member to take turns being the actor.

Pictionary

One team member draws a word or phrase and the rest of the team must guess what it is. Each member takes turns being the artist.

Jigsaw Puzzle

A puzzle of an equestrian topic such as the Pony Club poster on Poisonous plants to be put together. Points awarded for the number of pieces successfully put together. In 2024 one of the new PC posters will be used.

Taboo

Team members try to get their team mates to guess a word from clues they give, the only catch is that there is a list of words that are "taboo". Topic in 2024 Rugs and Boots/bandages.

Word Games

Alphabet Soup

Team members guess the word based on the letters of the alphabet and a clue.

Before and After

Two words are linked by a third word, the middle word must be linked to each of the original words but they do not have to link together. For example Silver _____ Guard the answer would be Buckle.

Crazy Horse Parts

A clue will give a point of anatomy or conformation. For example "What sits on a lily pad?" Answer would be Frog. Topic in 2024 points of the horse and conformation.

Crossword Puzzle

Find the answers to questions based on the number of letters and clues. Topic in 2024 Care of the foot (mini) and Feeding (J/S).

Hexagonal Cube

Match the words, to be based on the Blue Cross Mini and Achievement Badges.

Identification Rounds

Memory Test/Concentration

Look at items for 90sec then write down as many as possible. Topic in 2023 Grooming kit/First Aid.

Green Thumb

ID plants and trees from photos. Topic in 2024 Grasses, Trees and Poisonous Plants.

What's my Job

ID the job based on the clues given. Topic in 2024 Shoeing.

Odd One Out

ID the item/word not belonging in the category. Topic in 2024 Blue Cross Badges.

Zoomed In

Close up or funny angle photos of equestrian items. Topic in 2023 around the yard.

Points of the Horse

Pin the points on an image of horse.

Yard Safety

ID the hazards to be found in a yard photograph.

Points of Tack

Outline pictures of tack with labels to be filled in for the points.

What's my Name

ID items either in real life or from photos. Topic in 2024 Shoeing.

Healthy Horse/Pony

ID statements of good and poor health, correctly ID photos of good and poor condition horse/ponies.

Colours and Markings

ID the colours and markings presented in photos.

Tack Identify

Items of tack on table to be identified.

<u>Feeding</u>

Identify the feed samples by writing the item name against its number on the answer sheet. Answer the questions, place the answers on the answer sheet against each number.

52. APPENDIX D – PCIA QUIZ

The Pony Club International Alliance Quiz invites teams from all over the world each year to compete against other National Teams competing against each other to win the PCIA International Quiz.

Teams are made up of four members aged 16 years to 25 years old. The UK team is invited to apply for the team, and must meet the Eligibility Criteria below. Open invitations to apply are also possible to give everyone the opportunity to apply.

a. Eligibility Criteria:

- To be a current Pony Club Member at the time of application
- To have competed in Junior/Senior Quiz Final, and/or the Senior Horse and Pony Care Championships in the last 3 years
- To be under 25 years of age on the date of competition
- To currently hold their B Test or above

b. Application Process

Applications will be taken through a form, which is advertised on the PC website, through the PC Instagram, as well as send to DCs, Centre Proprietors and Area Representatives.

The application submission deadline will be clearly specified on the application form.

Each applicant must meet all of the required criteria.

Each applicant must submit an up-to-date CV and Personal Statement.

Each applicant must provide a reference from their DC/Centre Proprietor (if either are family then an appropriate alternative is acceptable).

Each applicant must provide another reference from an appropriate person, e.g. Quiz Team Manager, or Area Representative.

Applicants will then be shortlisted and invited for an interview, before the final 4 team members are selected. For an exchange, another member will be chosen as a 1st reserve in case one of the chosen members pulls out.

If it is an exchange, the members will be expected to raise funds for their trip. The approximate cost will be given on the application form so that members can decide whether they will be able to raise the amount needed.